EAR TRAINING FOR PRACTICAL EXAMINATIONS

MELODY PLAYBACK/SINGBACK 4

A COMPLETE COURSE OF EAR TESTS
FOR PRACTICAL EXAMINATIONS
BY

BORIS BERLIN and ANDREW MARKOW

Part One: Levels (Grades) 1 to 4
Part Two: Levels (Grades) 5 and 6
Part Three: Levels (Grades) 7 and 8
Part Four: Levels (Grades) 9 to 11 (Associateship)

ISBN 978-0-88797-251-5

Printed in Canada

INTRODUCTION

The purpose of this set of books is to provide a series of practical playback (singback) tests for both teachers and students. These tests meet the requirements of most examination systems, particularly those of the Royal Conservatory of Music, the Western Ontario Conservatory of Music, the Western Board and others. They are invaluable as the basis of a sound preparation for examinations and auditions and offer a wealth of material to be used in furthering a comprehensive musical development as well as in assessing current progress.

Since these tests are universal, students are advised to cover them thoroughly for their own over-all musical development and enrichment regardless of whether they take examinations or not.

The playback (singback) tests in these books cover all levels (grades) from one to eleven (Associateship) and, as in the case of the lower levels, comprise all the possible combinations as required for examinations. In general the tests consist of an extensive number of aural playbacks (singbacks) to be used in the musical development of all instrumentalists and vocalists and as such should be both sung back and played back on the respective instruments.

Groups of tests are designated by [A] , [B] and/or [C] . Tests designated by [A] correspond to the current requirements of the Royal Conservatory of Music, those by [B] to the requirements of the Western Ontario Conservatory of Music, and those by [C] to the requirements of the Western Board. Nevertheless, we strongly recommend that the current syllabus of each examining board be consulted for its respective requirements in each grade.

Boris Berlin
Andrew Markow

HOW TO USE THE BOOK

The purpose of these tests is to help the student prepare for the playback (singback) section of the ear test part of practical examinations as well as to develop musical memory, a sense of observation, aural recognition, playing by ear, an awareness of note patterns and shapes, a feeling for intervallic relationships, and a keen perception of melodic and rhythmic design.

For best results the students should cover at least one test DAILY by (1.) naming its key; (2.) playing the tonic chord; (3.) playing BOTH parts of the test TWICE while singing or humming the upper part for Level (Grade) 9, the lower part for Level (Grade) 10 and first the upper, then the lower part for Level (Grade) 11 (Associateship); and (4.) playing the part or parts back from memory. If necessary each step can be repeated until (4.) is attainable. The student should observe the DIRECTION of the notes, the PATTERNS they form and the over-all SHAPE of each part.

It is strongly recommended that the student practise the typical endings found on pages 3 and 4 using the procedure outlined above. In this way the student will become familiar with the sound and structure of various endings and find it easier to retain the entire phrase by memory.

The teacher will explain and illustrate how the phrase is structured; i.e. the way the notes move by step or by skip (intervals) to form patterns, scales, broken triads or chords, repeated notes, etc. The student's attention must also be drawn to changes in direction (up or down), the over-all design (shape) of the part or parts, the implied harmonies and the feeling of the rhythmic pattern.*

At the lesson the teacher should check the student's home practice by using the examination procedure: choosing one of the tests, naming the key and playing the tonic chord, and then playing the two-part phrase twice, asking the student to sing (intone or whistle) and/or play back the relevant part or parts. A parent, brother or sister, or a friend can also assist by giving tests using the same procedure.

By commencing at a lower level one builds progressively. Regardless of the level used, however, one should start at the beginning in order to achieve a good understanding and a solid foundation.

**See the set of books on rhythm in this series,* *Rhythm Clapback/Singback 1-3.*

LEVELS (GRADES) 9, 10, AND 11 (ASSOCIATESHIP)

Preliminary Exercises

A and **B**

Endings of Two-Part Phrases:

The following are examples of typical endings of two-part phrases in major and minor keys. These endings can occur in any key and in various rhythmic patterns. It is recommended that the student practise these endings in several different keys.

DIRECTIONS:

Name the key.
Play the tonic chord.
Play the phrase twice, observing the DIRECTION of the notes and the PATTERN they form.
For Level 9, SING or PLAY the UPPER PART without looking at the music.
For Level 10, SING or PLAY the LOWER PART without looking at the music.
For Level 11 (Associateship), PLAY BACK BOTH PARTS without looking at the music
(or sing one part while playing the other part).

A B
25 F major
26
27
28
29
30
B
31 D minor
32
33
34
35
36
A B
37 B♭ major
38
39
40
41
42
B
43 G minor
44
45
46
47
48
A B
49 D major
50
51
52
53
54
B
55 B minor
56
57
58
59
60

A and B

LEVEL 9 (GRADE 9)
Preliminary Exercises

Two-part phrases in a major key.

DIRECTIONS:
Name the key.
Play the tonic chord.
Play the phrase twice, observing the DIRECTION of the notes and the PATTERN they form.

A Play back the UPPER PART.

B Play back OR sing back (to any vowel) the UPPER PART.

Scale patterns

1 

2 

Intervals

3 

4 

Intervals and patterns by step

5 

6 

Repeated notes

7 

8 

Broken triads

9 

10 

Tests

Two-part phrases in a major key.

DIRECTIONS:
Name the key.
Play the tonic chord.
Play the phrase twice, observing the DIRECTION of the notes and the PATTERN they form.

A Play back the UPPER PART.

B Play back OR sing back (to any vowel) the UPPER PART.

1 

2 

3 

4 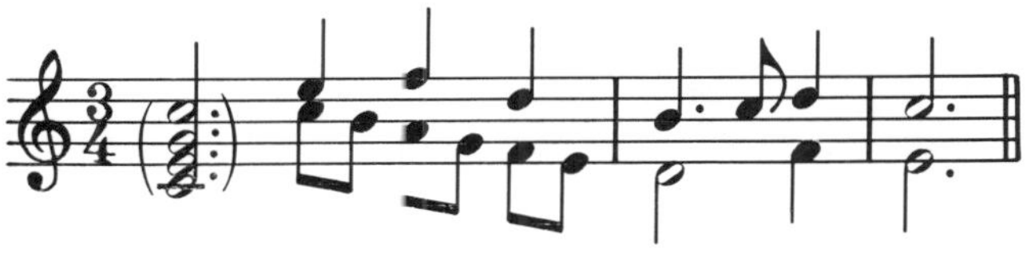

5

6

7

8

9
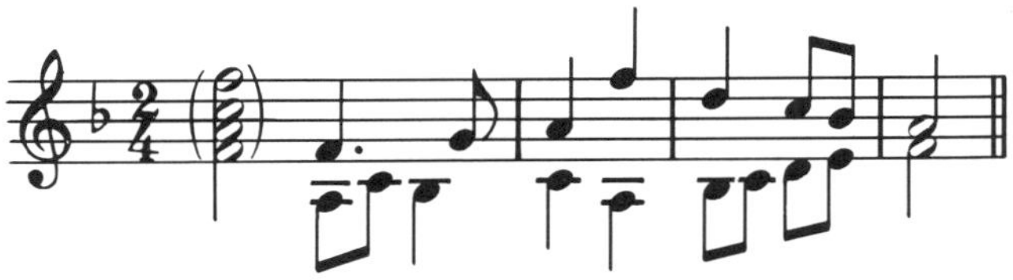

10

11

12

13

14

15

16

17

18

19

20

21
22
23
24
25
26
27
28
29
30
31
32
33
34
35
36

37

38

39

40

41

42

43
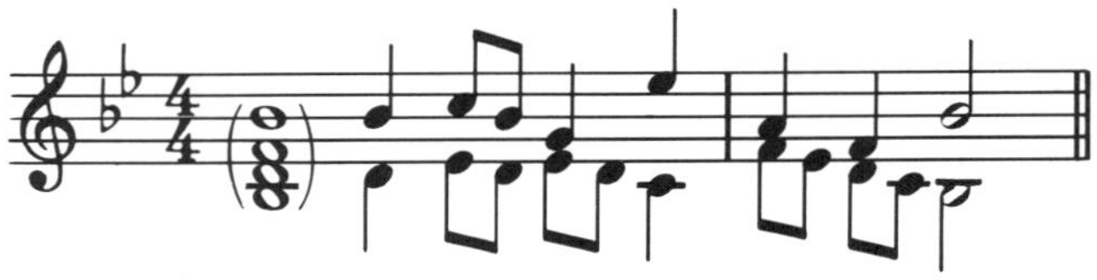

44

45

46

47

48

49

50

51

52

53

54

55

56

57

58

59

60

61

62

63

64

65

66

67

68

69

70

71

72

73

74
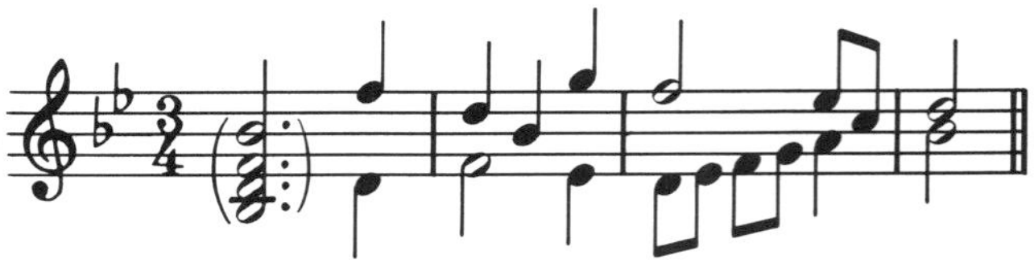

75

76

77

78

79

80

81
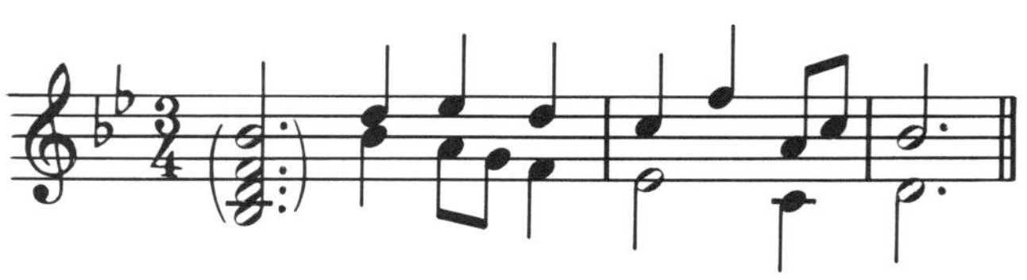

82
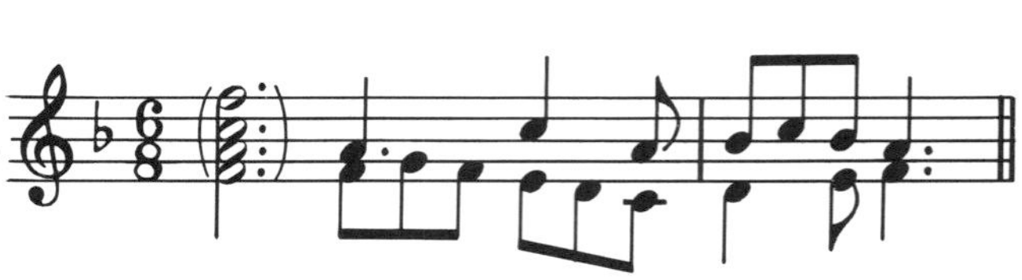

83

84

85 

86 

87 

88 

89 

90 

91 

92 

93 

94 

95 

96 

97 

98 

99 

100 

A and B

LEVEL 10 (GRADE 10)
Preliminary Exercises

Two-part phrases in a major key.

DIRECTIONS:
Name the key.
Play the tonic chord.
Play the phrase twice, observing the DIRECTION of the notes and the PATTERN they form.

A Play back the LOWER PART.

B Play back OR sing back (to any vowel) the LOWER PART.

Scale patterns

1 

2 

Intervals

3 

4 

Intervals and patterns by step

5 

6 

Repeated notes

7 

8 

Broken triads

9 

10 

Tests

Two-part phrases in a major key.

DIRECTIONS:
Name the key.
Play the tonic chord.
Play the phrase twice, observing the DIRECTION of the notes and the PATTERN they form.

A Play back the LOWER PART.

B Play back OR sing back (to any vowel) the LOWER PART.

1 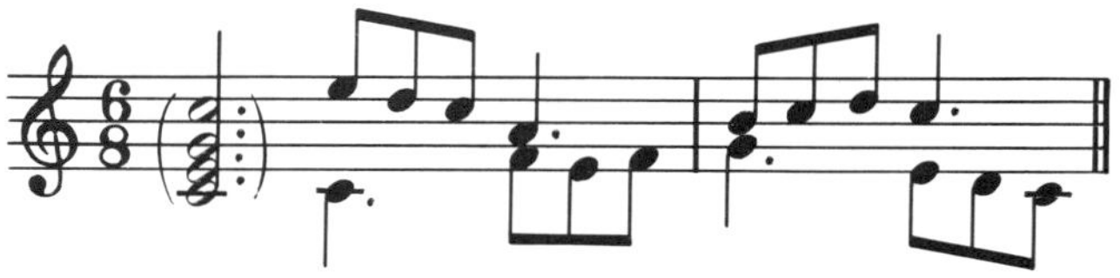

2 

3 

4 

21 

22 

23 

24 

25 

26 

27 

28 

29 

30 

31 

32 

33 

34 

35 

36 

37
38
39
40
41
42
43
44
45
46
47
48
49
50
51
52

53 

54 

55 

56 

57 

58 

59 

60 

61 

62 

63 

64 

65 

66 

67 

68 

69

70

71

72

73

74

75

76

77

78

79

80

81

82

83

84

85

86

87

88

89

90

91

92

93

94

95

96

97

98

99

100

A and B

LEVEL 11 (GRADE 11) (ASSOCIATESHIP)

Preliminary Exercises

Two-part phrases in a major key.

DIRECTIONS:
Name the key.
Play the tonic chord.
Play the phrase twice, observing the DIRECTION of the notes and the PATTERN they form.

A and B Play back BOTH parts.

Patterns in parallel motion

1 

2 

Patterns in contrary motion

3 

4 

Broken triads or chords

5 

6 

Repeated notes

7 

8 

Imitation

9 

10 

Tests

Two-part phrases in a major key.

DIRECTIONS:
Name the key.
Play the tonic chord.
Play the phrase twice, observing the DIRECTION of the notes and the PATTERN they form.

A and B Play back BOTH parts.

1 

2 

3 

4 

5 

6 

7 

8 

9 

10 

11 

12 

13 

14 

15 

16 

17 

18 

19 

20 

21 

22 

23 

24 

25 

26 

27 

28 

29 

30 

31 

32 

33 

34 

35 

36 

37
38
39
40
41
42
43
44
45
46
47
48
49
50
51
52

53 

54 

55 

56 

57 

58 

59 

60 

61 

62 

63 

64 

65 

66 

67 

68 

69

70

71

72

73

74

75

76

77

78

79

80

81

82

83

84

85 

86 

87 

88 

89 

90 

91 

92 

93 

94 

95 

96 

97 

98 

99 

100 

B LEVEL 11 (GRADE 11) (ASSOCIATESHIP) continued

Preliminary Exercises

Two-part phrases in a minor key.

DIRECTIONS:
Name the key.
Play the tonic chord.
Play the phrase twice, observing the DIRECTION of the notes and the PATTERN they form.

B Play back BOTH parts.

Patterns in parallel motion

1 

2 

Patterns in contrary motion

3 

4 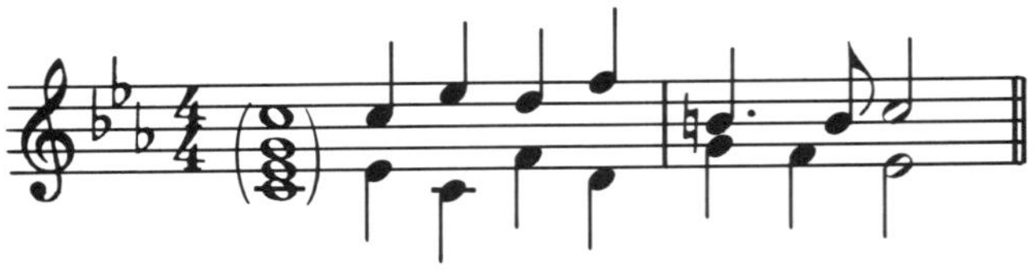

Intervals

5 

6 

Broken triads or chords

7 

8 

Repeated notes

9 

10 

Imitation

11 

12 

Tests

Two-part phrases in a minor key.

DIRECTIONS:
Name the key.
Play the tonic chord.
Play the phrase twice, observing the DIRECTION of the notes and the PATTERN they form.

B Play back BOTH parts.

1 

2 

3 

4 

5

6

7

8

9

10

11

12

13

14

15

16

17

18

19

20

21 

22 

23 

24 

25 

26 

27 

28 

29 

30 

31 

32 

33 

34 

35 

36 

37 

38 

39 

40 

41 

42 

43 

44 

45 

46 

47 

48 

49 

50 

51 

52 

53 

54 

55 

56 

57 

58 

59 

60 

61 

62 

63 

64 

65 

66 

67 

68 

69

70

71

72

73

74

75

76

77

78

79

80

81

82

83

84

85

86

87

88

89

90

91

92

93

94

95

96

97

98

99

100